CONTENTS

Some words are printed in bold, **like this.** You can find out what they mean by looking in the glossary.

For many people tennis is a great game to play or watch in the summer. For some people, tennis is far more than just a game. For a young boy growing up in Scotland in the 1990s, tennis became his life. He was determined to make tennis his career and his ambition was to be a world champion.

Andy Murray's amazing rise to the top of his sport came from hard work, skill, and determination. His parents supported him all the way and even when he was still at school, people noticed him. In 2002, at the age of 15, he made his Junior Wimbledon **debut**. Two years later Andy was picked for Britain's **Davis Cup** team. By the time he was 17, Andy Murray's name was known around the world.

Since becoming a **professional** tennis player in 2005, Andy Murray has become one of the best players in the sport. By the beginning of 2008, Andy was the 9th best tennis player in the world.

FAST FACT FILE

Name:	Andrew Murray
Born:	15 May 1987, Glasgow, Scotland
Height:	1.90 m (6 ft 3 in)
Weight:	79 kg (174 lb)
Family:	Mum Judy, dad William, brother Jamie
Started playing:	Started playing tennis aged three
Turned professional:	2005
Plays:	Right-handed; two-handed backhand
Highest world ranking:	9 (January 2008)
Charity:	Supergrounds

Could Andy Murray be the next British winner of Wimbledon?

Did you know?

No British man has won the Wimbledon Men's Singles title since Fred Perry in 1936. Since then, Great Britain has been waiting for a tennis star to repeat Perry's great success. Could Andy Murray be the one to do it? The former world number one tennis player John McEnroe said of Andy: "With Andy, the sky's the limit." Many people hope and believe that Andy can win Wimbledon.

Andy Murray was born in 1987 in Glasgow, Scotland. He and his older brother, Jamie, grew up in a town called Dunblane, next to the town's sports club. The tennis courts next door were a great place to play, even as toddlers. Judy, their mother, was a keen tennis player and was a tennis **coach** at the club.

While their mother taught people how to improve their game, Andy (on the left) and his older brother, Jamie, played against each other.

WHO IS ANDY'S MUM?

Judy Murray is the mother and manager of tennis star Andy Murray. She was also a tennis champion. She won 64 Scottish titles and worked as the Scottish national tennis coach between 1995 and 2004. She has great hopes for both her sons in international tennis. Her biggest hope for Andy is to see him lift the Men's Singles trophy at Wimbledon one day!

Andy started playing tennis at the age of three and says: "I know for sure that I had a mini racket when I was two. I used to knock sponge balls off the walls in the house until my mum got fed up with it and got a swing-ball for the back garden." When still very young, Andy and Jamie learned how to hit tennis balls across a full-size court, and over a net that was the same height as they were!

By the time he was about eight years old, Andy was hooked on tennis. As they got older, Andy and Jamie competed in local under-10 competitions. Jamie was the older brother, and at first he was the better player, winning more matches. But playing against an older brother quickly helped to improve Andy's tennis. It also made him very competitive and desperate to win.

Andy's mum, Judy, encouraged him and his brother to take up tennis.

Andy had great opportunities as a child, but his early years weren't all fun and games. There were difficult times for Andy during the 1990s. During this time his parents split up. He recalled, "I would get really upset, and one of the things I would have loved to have more than anything was a family that worked better together, although I love my mother and father to bits."

Tragedy

Andy went to Dunblane Primary School where, when he was eight years old, something horrific happened. A gunman walked into the school and began shooting. The attack happened just as year one pupils were starting a lesson in the gym. Sixteen children and a teacher died.

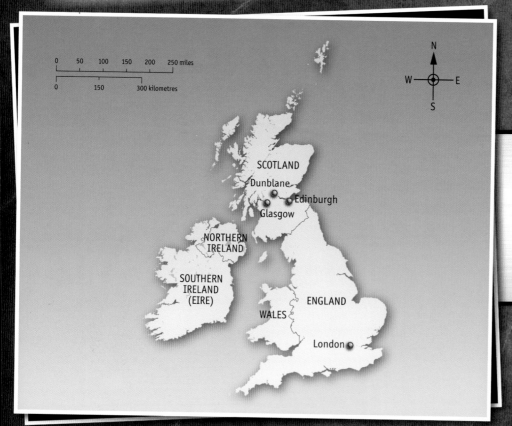

Dunblane is a town of 10,000 people, 64 kilometres (40 miles) from Edinburgh.

Dunblane School went through a tragic time in 1996.

Today, Andy doesn't remember much about the shooting. "I knew the guy who did the shooting, we all went to his boys' clubs. I was young at the time and didn't realise how it was a really difficult time for the town. But I think everyone has recovered well from it and the town has moved on."

The school closed for a while and the town mourned the children and teacher who had died. "I was just conscious of this great sadness in the town," Andy remembered. Did such a shocking experience affect him at all? "Sometimes I wonder if it shaped me in some way, helped to make me the person I am – more determined to do something with my life. Certainly I hope I can do something for Dunblane. I hope I can make the town famous for something else, other than tragedy."

Andy concentrated on throwing himself into tennis and improving his skills. "When I was younger and went on court, I could just go out and play."

Between the ages of 11 and 13, Andy played on a junior tennis team at the Next Generation club in Newhaven, Edinburgh. At this time Andy's tennis was really improving and he won his first big tournament: the Orange Bowl tournament in Florida, USA. It was 1999 and Andy was just 12 years old.

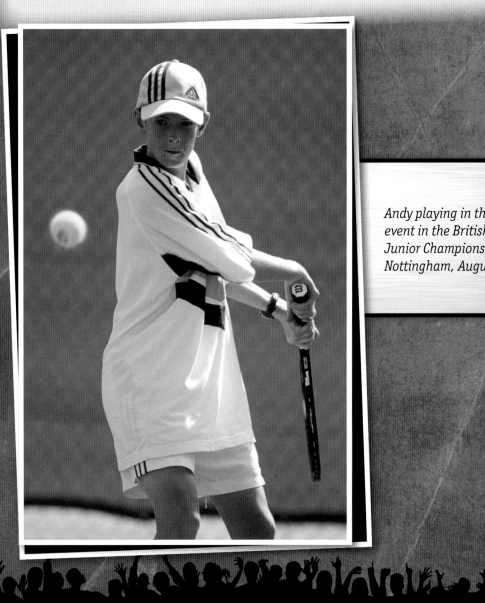

Andy playing in the under 14s event in the British National Junior Championships, Nottingham, August 1999.

Although he was doing well and his game was improving, Andy and his mother felt that he wasn't learning the game fast enough. Andy wanted more than the local tennis clubs and schools could offer. Andy's family had heard of a famous school that specialised in tennis training – the only problem was that it was in Spain! At the age of 15, Andy went to live more than 1,609 kilometres (1,000 miles) away from his family home. He attended the Sánchez-Casal tennis **academy** in Barcelona. Andy later said the move abroad helped to make him more independent and allowed him to focus on his dream.

THE SANCHEZ - CASAL ACADEMY

This school is especially for young tennis players. Students get top-level tennis training, as well as study time (all in English). Students spend three hours each day having on-court training and one hour each day working on their fitness.

They also have:
- a developed, personalised playing pattern
- **tactical** work in three areas of on-court play
- a personal technical tutor
- **psychological** follow-up
- a personalised competition programme
- **coach**-managed games.

Such a training academy wouldn't suit everyone, but it seemed to work for Andy. Maybe another reason why he enjoyed his time at Barcelona was because it's a lot warmer and drier than Dunblane!

In September 2004, when Andy was 17 he won the US Open Boys' Singles title. It was a great win for Andy. Two weeks later, he was asked to represent Great Britain in the **Davis Cup** against Austria, although he didn't get to play. Despite the disappointment, there was another high point in 2004, when Andy was awarded BBC Young Sports Personality of the Year.

In March 2005, Andy was again asked to join the Great Britain Davis Cup team. This time he got to play and played with David Sherwood in a doubles match. They won and helped Britain to a 3-2 victory.

Winning the US Open Boys' Singles title in September 2004 was a great boost to Andy's junior career.

Turning professional

Andy turned **professional** in May 2005, just after his 18th birthday. This meant he became a full-time player with the Association of Tennis Professionals (**ATP**) organizing all his tournaments throughout the year. He was now able to compete in tournaments where the top prizes ranged from £250,000 to over £1 million!

A few weeks after turning professional, Andy played in his first senior **Grand Slam** tournament – Wimbledon. He was **ranked** 374th in the world, but he reached the third round. He was eventually beaten by David Nalbandian after a long match. After leading by two sets to love, Andy became very tired in the fourth and fifth sets. After this match people wondered whether Andy was physically fit enough to win long matches.

AN EASY LIFE?

The life of a tennis player isn't an easy one. Travelling around the world and playing in different tournaments means that players are away from their family and friends for long periods of time. Playing matches, practising, and training in the gym are all hard work and there's not much time for anything else.

Professional tennis players earn their money by winning tournaments through **sponsors**, and through deals with clothing manufacturers. If a player performs badly, they can lose a lot of money. However, some tournaments offer "appearance money" or give presents to players during the competition, such as a car or free meals at top restaurants. So there are some compensations.

What is it like for brothers who are both **professional** tennis players? Andy and his older brother Jamie are very competitive. Jamie always used to beat Andy at tennis when they were young. Then Andy started to come out on top. Andy once said, "Tennis is the only thing that I'm better at than him. He is cleverer than me, studied harder than me, and was better at athletics. Today he's more supportive than anyone."

Jamie has also said a few things about his younger brother! He was about 10 years old when Andy first beat him. "I wasn't happy. We were playing in the same age categories by then, but nothing prepares for you for it! We were still quite competitive after that, but when he was 15 he went to Spain to train. When he came back, he was a lot better."

Then, in 2007, Jamie said about his successful younger brother, "I'm obviously very proud of Andy, but I've also worked really hard and my own career is starting to take off. We're together most weeks now, so it's like we've come full circle."

When Jamie was asked about Andy's most irritating habit, he said it was stubbornness. "If you asked him what he disliked about me, it would be interrupting his stories!"

JAMIE MURRAY

Jamie Murray (born 13 February 1986) plays in doubles, and has been the UK number one in the **ATP** doubles **rankings**. His nickname is "Stretch" because his long arms seem able to stretch right out to reach balls at the net. Jamie won the mixed doubles final of Wimbledon in 2007 with Jelena Jankovic, from Serbia.

*Although he prefers to play singles, Andy Murray has said that he would be more proud winning a doubles **Grand Slam** with Jamie than winning a singles Grand Slam on his own.*

DOUBLES

Singles matches are shown on television far more than doubles. However, there have been some great doubles partnerships such as John McEnroe and Peter Fleming from the United States, and Todd Woodbridge and Mark Woodforde from Australia. Andy does sometimes play doubles matches, but generally the two brothers keep to their own styles of tennis.

Any world-class tennis player has to keep at top fitness throughout the year in order to take part in the major events around the world. Although Andy plays in many tournaments during the year, it's important for him to do well in the four big events that make up the **Grand Slam**. A "Grand Slam" is winning all the Grand Slams in any one year. A "Career Grand Slam" is winning all four in a lifetime.

GRAND SLAMS

These four tournaments last for two weeks each year:

Australian Open – January at Melbourne Park.

French Open – mid-May and early June in Paris, at the Stade de Roland Garros.

Wimbledon – late June and early July at the All England Lawn Tennis and Croquet Club in London.

US Open – August and September at the USTA Billie Jean King National Tennis Center at Flushing Meadows, at Corona Park, New York City.

Wimbledon

Andy likes playing at Wimbledon because the home crowd cheers him on. "I really enjoy Wimbledon. I really look forward to it every year and obviously having all of the people in the stadium wanting you to win is pretty special." Even so, he's suggested that it's not his favourite tournament and that he prefers the US Open. It uses **hard courts**, unlike Wimbledon that has **grass courts**. Other players prefer **clay courts** to the grass courts of Wimbledon.

For many years people in Britain hoped that Tim Henman would win Wimbledon. When he retired from playing tennis in September 2007, Andy Murray became the next British hope.

Fans gather on what has become known as "Henman Hill" to watch Tim Henman play tennis. Many people now refer to the hill as "Murray Mound".

ANDY MURRAY'S BEST GRAND SLAM RESULTS

Australian Open:	2009, fourth round
French Open:	2008, third round
Wimbledon Open:	2008, quarter final
US Open:	2008, final

To find out Andy's latest world ranking, go to
http://www.atptennis.com/1/en/home
Click on "Rankings" and then "Full ATP rankings".

Causing a Stir

No one likes to lose and all tennis players are competitive. Some people say that Andy Murray can be aggressive on the court. They say that he should be more in control of himself when things don't go his way. At times Andy has become so cross in matches that he has been known to shout at the umpire.

Andy admits: "I'm a bit fiery on court, but I'm always going to be like that and I don't want to change. If I don't get annoyed on court I don't play well, so I'm not goingto stop it just because a few people don't like it."

Andy reacts angrily after losing a point against Jonas Bjorkman of Sweden at the 2007 US Open tennis tournament in New York.

Bad press

When Andy shouts too much, headlines appear in newspapers about his temper. Andy was once fined £1,268 ($2,500) for calling the umpire names after microphones picked up what he said. Andy believed a shot from his opponent was out and he was furious that the umpire didn't agree. After arguing with the umpire, Andy was **jeered** by some of the crowd. They thought that he should just keep on playing.

When so much is at stake in top matches, it's not surprising players can lose their cool. After all, results affect **ranking** – and that's a serious business. But, like other sportspeople in the public eye, players have to be careful what they say, in case their words are taken the wrong way.

FOR THE RECORD

Every male player starts each year with zero points. Their best 18 performances of the year are awarded points. If a player misses a tournament he cannot earn points from it that year. Whichever player has the most points at the end of the season is the world number one – the best male tennis player in the world. Rankings are updated each week.

In April 2007 Andy Murray became the tenth best player in the world, after Tommy Haas failed to reach the US Men's **Clay Court** Championships semi-finals.

Sports stars are always in the news. People like to keep up-to-date with the latest results; they also like to know all about the lives of the best-known sports men and women. Having everything you do and say reported in the papers is all part of being famous, but it must take some getting used to. Andy has given many interviews and some have revealed quite a lot about him. He has also taken the opportunity to express his views, such as what he thinks about the poor behaviour of some younger tennis players.

Andy warns British youngsters

In 2007, the **Lawn Tennis Association** stopped supporting a few junior tennis players who had been boasting about their wild nights out. Andy said that Britain's young players must be more focused if they are to have any success in tennis. When the juniors were **suspended** for "unprofessional behaviour", Andy said: "Everyone goes through a phase like this – I made mistakes at 16 when I was in Barcelona. But now I don't drink, I don't smoke – it's the sacrifice you have to make if you want to become a great athlete." Andy added that **professional** athletes have to realise they're not in a nine-to-five job and they have to stay in the best shape possible at all times. "Being professional is the main thing you need to get right. If you don't have that then you're never going to make it."

Finding the right coach

The American **coach** Brad Gilbert began coaching Andy in July 2006. They parted just over a year later. Andy said: "Despite being injured for almost four months, I am pleased with my 2007 results. But the time has come to move on. I am **ranked** 11 in the world and can now afford to hire a team of experts in the development of my tennis and fitness." This fitness team includes former player Miles Maclagan, who is acting as Andy's main coach.

Even top sportspeople are sometimes allowed to eat cake – but only on special occasions, such as Jamie's 21st birthday!

The more successful a sports star becomes, the more offers come in from big companies. Fame is often a path to fortune because many companies feel that a well-known face that's famous for winning has the power to sell their products. Andy Murray has the opportunity to earn millions of pounds from **sponsors**. By wearing their clothes, using their equipment, or just showing a **logo** when he appears in front of the cameras, Andy gets paid very well.

SPONSORSHIP

All top players earn sponsorship money from companies by wearing logos on their tennis clothes. Players are also paid to wear a particular brand of tennis clothes and shoes, such as Nike, Yonex, Fila, or Adidas, as well as to use a particular brand of racket such as Wilson, Babolat, or Slazenger. Andy Murray promotes Fred Perry clothing and he uses a custom-made Head racket with the company's logo. But if Andy has a bad time and his position falls, the sponsors may start to look elsewhere. Lower **ranked** players don't get offered such great deals.

The face

Andy has agreed to be "the face of David Lloyd Leisure", a sports and health club. The company hopes Andy's advertising will encourage young children to take up tennis.

The left sleeve

Highland Spring signed one of the biggest deals in tennis history for a small logo on Andy's shirt sleeve. The **contract**, worth over £1 million, also requires Andy to take part in special events and to drink the company's bottled water – in front of millions.

The watch

Swiss watch company Tag Heuer signed a deal with Andy to wear one of their watches at sporting events. Now he can't afford to turn up late!

The book

To add to Andy's fame and fortune, his **autobiography** tells his own story so far. Publicity quotes such as this show how much interest there is in Andy: "The boy from Dunblane tells about dealing with the constant limelight and a media desperate for a genuine British tennis star."

Andy has the logos of his sponsors on his tennis clothes and equipment.

Like many sportspeople, Andy Murray has been able to use some of his fame and fortune to help others. Andy and his **sponsor**, The Royal Bank of Scotland (RBS), have supported a scheme to get children interested and involved in sport.

Both Andy and Jamie are involved with the Supergrounds scheme and they visit primary schools to promote "getting active". Supergrounds is a £6 million, six-year programme, funded by RBS to develop primary school playgrounds into exciting places to learn and play safely. "Kids these days are not getting enough exercise, so I think the money that RBS is investing in Supergrounds can definitely make a difference."

Andy launches "Supergrounds" at a school. He says, "It's a great way to get kids to lead a more active lifestyle and make the most of their playgrounds."

Another of Andy and Jamie's projects is "12 things to do before you're 12". It is hoped that this project will help to get children actively involved with sport.

In 2007, Andy also launched his "Road to Andy Murray" project to encourage children to play tennis. He feels that the programme is "a fantastic way to encourage kids to play their best tennis while having fun. This is great for the British game."

Andy raised £10,000 having his hair cut live on television for the 2006 Children in Need appeal – quite a snip!

BAD HAIR DAY

Being famous and always in the public eye can be difficult. After all, everyone expects you to look your best all the time. Would you believe that at one time Andy didn't get his hair cut **professionally** for 18 months? Instead, he sometimes took out his frustration after a bad match by cutting it himself! He once cut off so much hair that it filled a litter bin! "I was pretty angry so I went back to my hotel and I filled up my whole bin." Maybe that's why Andy chose to have his hair cut in public to raise more than £10,000 for Children in Need, a charity that aims to raise money to help disadvantaged children.

Challenges ahead

Who can tell what Andy Murray's future will be in world-class tennis? The pressure is on him to become the next British champion, but his success will depend on many things, such as his level of skill, fitness, and **stamina**. Sudden strains, cramps, and health problems can stop an athlete from competing. Andy has already had to pull out of tournaments after damaging his wrist.

When asked if he had any targets for the future, he replied: "I just want to keep improving. With still being young, I'm going to get fitter and stronger as well." Andy has also said, "If I stay fit and healthy, I will have a good chance at one of the **Grand Slams**." That's one of his big challenges ahead.

Roger Federer is one of the top tennis stars to beat.

THE TOP MAN

Six years older than Andy, Roger Federer is a Swiss tennis player who has **ranked** World Number 1 for a record number of years. Roger has won three Grand Slam singles titles in a year three times (in 2004, 2006, and 2007). That's a record! He is the only male player to have played in the finals of all four Grand Slam tournaments for two years running. By winning Wimbledon in 2007, he achieved five Wimbledon championships in a row. Andy has a tough challenge to beat Roger – but he's up for it!

Whether or not Andy Murray ever beats Roger Federer, he will surely continue to win many top titles in world tennis. He may not win a Grand Slam tournament yet, but there are plenty of interesting challenges ahead.

Andy was one of a number of sports stars who helped unveil the new London 2012 logo for the Olympic and Paralympic games. He is already looking ahead to playing at London 2012: "I would love to get the chance to play. To be the face of the Olympics would be awesome."

Andy might even get to win a gold medal in the London Olympics! For as he once said "I'm not really too sure what I love about tennis – I just enjoy winning." You can bet the winning is likely to continue for many years yet.

1987	Andy is born in Glasgow.
1999	Andy wins the Under-12s Orange Bowl world championships, Florida, USA.
2002	Andy's Junior Wimbledon **debut**.
2004	Andy wins the Junior Men's Singles title at the US Open and goes on to become the 2004 BBC Young Sports Personality of the Year (aged 17).
2005	Andy becomes Britain's youngest **Davis Cup** player when he plays against Israel.
	In May 2005, aged 18, Andy turns **professional**.
	On 20 June 2005 Andy is **ranked** 312. A couple of days later, he defeats 14th seed Radek Stepanek at Wimbledon. He rises 99 places to 213th in the **ATP** rankings, making him the sixth highest-placed Briton.
2006	Andy beats Lleyton Hewitt in the final of the **SAP** Open in San Jose.
	At the age of 18 years and 9 months Andy becomes the fourth youngest tennis player to win an ATP competition. The result raises his world ranking to 47th. He hires the highly-rated Brad Gilbert as a **coach**.
2007	Andy reaches the final of the Qatar Open and gains a career-high world ranking of 15th.
	Andy retains his SAP Open title in San Jose. He becomes a top 10 player after his rival for 10th place, Tommy Haas, fails to reach the US **Clay Court** Championships semi-finals.
2008	Andy is seeded ninth at the 2008 Australian Open, his first time in the Top 10 seeds at a Grand Slam. He loses in the first round to the eventual finalist, Jo-Wilfried Tsonga.
	Andy wins five titles in the year.
	Andy reaches the final of a Grand Slam for the first time. He loses to Rafael Nadal in the final of the US Open.
2009	Andy begins 2009 with his highest career ranking of 4th.
	Andy wins his 10th career title, beating world number 3, Novak Djokovic, at the Sony Ericsson Open in Miami, USA. Andy has equalled former British tennis player Tim Henman's career total of 11 titles.

Amazing facts

- Andy is also good at other sports, including karting, golf, and football. He once said "I actually dabbled in a bit of football with Glasgow Rangers, but it didn't last. It was always going to be the tennis."

- In March 2005, when Andy played on Great Britain's Davis Cup team against Israel, he became the youngest ever British player to play in a Davis Cup match.

- Andy's ex-coach Brad Gilbert previously coached the American, Andre Agassi.

- Andy has vowed to sign autographs for every fan who asks him to. This is because once, when he went to watch his idol Andre Agassi play at Wimbledon, he asked Andre for his autograph and Andre ignored him.

- Andy's hero is Mohammad Ali.

- Andy's favourite films include: *Wedding Crashers, Braveheart,* and *Oceans 11.*

Glossary

academy place for training in special subjects or skills

ATP Association of Tennis Professionals (it is made up of only male professionals)

autobiography person's life story that is written by that person

clay court red tennis court made of crushed shale or brick. A clay court is "slower" court, because the balls bounce higher and more slowly.

coach someone who teaches a sport

contract agreement between two people. In tennis, a player usually signs a contract in which they agree to use a certain product in exchange for money.

Davis Cup international team event in men's tennis, run by the International Tennis Federation

debut first public appearance playing sport

Grand Slam the four big tennis tournments held round the world each year. Each one lasts for two weeks.

grass court Wimbledon is the only Grand Slam tournament played on grass. A grass court is faster to play on than a clay or a hard court.

hard court tennis court made out of cement or asphalt (pitch or tar). A hard court plays slower than a grass court but faster than a clay court.

jeer shout things at someone

Lawn Tennis Association (LTA) governing body for the game of tennis in Great Britain

logo symbol used for easy recognition of a company

professional doing something to earn money

psychological to do with thinking and the mind

ranking put in order of how good someone is compared with other people

SAP started in 1889, the second oldest men's professional tennis tournament in the United States

sponsor give money in order to fund a project or team

stamina being able to work hard over a long time. If a tennis player has good stamina they are able to play well for a long match.

suspend stop someone doing something for a time

tactic carefully planned strategy or action

Useful address

The Lawn Tennis Association, The National Tennis Centre, 100 Priory Lane, Roehampton, London SW15 5JQ. Tel: 020 8487 7000

Websites

http://www.andymurray.com/
Find out more about Andy Murray at his official website. You can find up-to-date news and see his current world ranking.

http://www.lta.org.uk/
On this site you can find out where your nearest tennis club is and discover more about tennis in Britain.

http://www.supergrounds.com/index.aspx
Visit this site to learn more about the charity Supergrounds, which Andy Murray supports.

http://www.wimbledon.org/en_GB/index.html
This site has everything you need to know about the Wimbledon tournament.

Books

Andrew Murray: Wonderboy, Euan Reedie (John Blake Publishing Ltd, 2006)

Andy Murray: The Story So Far..., Rob Robertson & Eleanor Preston (Mainstream Publishing, 2006)

Hitting Back, Andy Murray (Century, 2008)

Tim Henman: England's Finest, Simon Felstein (John Blake Publishing Ltd, 2006)

Disclaimer

All the Internet addresses (URLs) given in this book were valid at the time of going to press. However, due to the dynamic nature of the Internet, some addresses may have changed, or sites may have changed or ceased to exist since publication. While the author and Publishers regret any inconvenience this may cause readers, no responsibility for any such changes can be accepted by either the author or the Publishers. It is recommended that adults supervise children on the Internet.